Hey, Be and See

Hey, Be and See

We can be the change
we want to see in the world

Dave Andrews

Authentic

Copyright © 2010 Dave Andrews

16 15 14 13 12 11 10   7 6 5 4 3 2 1

First published 2010 by Authentic Media Limited
Milton Keynes
www.authenticmedia.co.uk

British Library Cataloguing in Publication Data

A catalogue record for this book is available from the British Library

ISBN-13: 978-1-85078-848-5

Cover design by Paul Airy, Four-Nine-Zero Design
(www.fourninezerodesign.co.uk)
Printed and bound in the UK by J. F. Print Ltd., Sparkford, Somerset

'The kingdom of heaven is here now
in the midst of you.'[1]
Jesus of Nazareth

'Have thy heart in Heaven
And thy hands on Earth;
Ascend in piety,
And descend in charity,
This is the nature of light
And the children of it.'[2]
Thomas Vaughan

'Who has not found Heaven below
Will fail of it above.
God's residence is next to mine,
(Its) furniture is love.'[3]
Emily Dickenson

'Love seeketh not itself to please
Nor for itself hath any care,
But for another gives its ease,
And builds a Heaven in Hell's despair.'[4]
William Blake

Contents

Introduction

The longer I live,
the less and less
I believe –
but
the little I believe in,
I believe in
more and more.

I love catching up with friends over a cup of tea.

It's a chance to take time out, swap stories, compare notes, and get some much-needed encouragement for the next stage of the journey. By the time we get round to the second or third cup of tea, we often find ourselves talking about faith - about how our lives have been influenced by our beliefs - and, in turn, how they have affected our beliefs.

As a result of these conversations I have come to realize that the longer I live, the less I believe - but the little that I do believe in, I believe in more and more. There's a whole lot I used to believe - that I used to talk about day and night - that I just don't talk about anymore. I couldn't care less about these things - whether or not they're true doesn't make any difference to me. But there is one thing, among the many things I used to believe, that I still believe - and that I still talk about as passionately as ever before - and that is the gospel embodied in the person of Jesus of Nazareth.

It is in the context of the gospel of Jesus that we can begin to truly appreciate the importance of *Plan Be* - that we can begin to truly appreciate the importance of embodying the Be-Attitudes in the context of a world characterized by poverty and violence. And it is also in the context of the gospel of Jesus that we can begin to get a glimpse of some of the implications of *Plan Be*. For in embodying the Be-Attitudes we can actually do God's will 'on earth as it is in heaven', and in doing God's will we can actually embody something of heaven in the midst of 'hell's despair'.

Hey, we can be the change we want to see in the world.

Dave Andrews
Brisbane 2009

Part One

The Kingdom
Of Heaven
Can Be Ours

Most Christians feel confident about two things: one, we know the gospel; and two, we know we need to simply proclaim the gospel, as best we can, in word and in deed. But I'm not sure about either of those things anymore.

What is the 'gospel'? Well, the word 'gospel' comes from the old English 'godspel', meaning 'good news'. So I guess we can say the gospel is the 'good news' of Jesus. But what is the 'good news' of Jesus? Recently I asked a national conference of full-time Christian evangelists, who had been preaching the 'gospel' faithfully day and night for years, to tell me their understanding of the 'good news' of Jesus. As you can imagine, everyone had lots of great ideas about the 'good news'. But not a single one of them told me what the 'gospel' was according to Jesus!

In the Bible there are four books containing four versions of the gospel story. And the one thing that they all agree on is this: the 'gospel' according to Jesus is all about 'the kingdom of God' – or, as it is sometimes called, 'the kingdom of heaven'. Matthew says that Jesus went throughout Galilee teaching in the synagogues and preaching 'the good news of the kingdom' (Matt. 4:23). Luke says that Jesus said, 'I must preach the good news of the kingdom of God, because that is why I was sent' (Luke 4:43). And Mark records Jesus saying: 'The time has come . . . The kingdom of God is near. Repent and believe the good news!' (Mark 1:15).

Jesus' core message is 'the gospel of the kingdom'. That's why Jesus began his famous Sermon on the Mount with the words 'Blessed are the poor in spirit, for theirs is the kingdom of heaven' (Matt. 5:3). In this sermon Jesus calls on his disciples to 'seek first the kingdom', to make it a priority, and to continually pray that the 'kingdom come . . . on earth as it is in heaven' (Matt. 6:33, 10). Throughout his ministry Jesus constantly preached and taught about 'the kingdom'. All of his parables are basically earthy stories about 'the kingdom of heaven'.

At the end of his ministry, after his spectacular death and miraculous resurrection, all Jesus wants to talk about is 'the kingdom'. Luke says that, 'After his suffering, Jesus showed himself to the disciples and gave many convincing proofs that he was alive. He appeared to them over a period of forty days and spoke about the kingdom of God' (Acts 1:3).

Only John records Jesus saying anything about being 'born again' – twice on one occasion. Matthew, Mark, and Luke never record Jesus saying anything about being 'born again' at all. But all of the gospel writers record Jesus speaking about the 'kingdom of God' again and again – some one hundred and fourteen times![5]

The Kingdom

Interestingly enough, Jesus never defines 'the kingdom'. Instead, he describes it so we can experience it whether we fully understand the theology behind 'the kingdom' or not. The first way Jesus unpacks 'the kingdom' is through his *parables*. Jesus says 'the kingdom of God' is like a seed that grows inside us. It starts small but grows big. It brings life, new life, with fresh thoughts and beautiful feelings, like flowers. And it makes our lives really fruitful. Many of us feel lost, but Jesus says 'the kingdom' is wherever a good shepherd finds the sheep that are lost, and whenever lost children find themselves again in the arms of a loving parent who gladly welcomes them and happily restores their broken and battered souls (Luke 15).

The second way Jesus unpacks 'the kingdom' is through his *relationships*. Jesus advocates a 'kingdom of friends for all those who feel friendless'. The Pharisees noted with disgust that 'This man welcomes sinners and eats with them' (Luke 15:2). But Jesus ignores their disdain and says to those weary with bearing the weight of public disapproval, 'Come to me, all you who are weary and burdened, and I will give you rest' (Matt. 12:28).

The third way Jesus unpacks 'the kingdom' is through his *responses*. Jesus advocates a kingdom of dreams come true – where there is real healing for the sick, the disturbed and distressed. One evening 'after sunset the people brought to Jesus all the sick and demon-possessed. The whole town gathered at the door, and Jesus healed many who had various diseases. He also drove out many demons' (Mark 1:32–34).

The fourth way Jesus unpacks 'the kingdom' is through his *example*. Jesus embodies the kingdom of a king who does not want to be a king. Knowing that they intended to come and make him king, 'Jesus withdrew again to a mountain by himself' (John 6:15). Jesus insisted that 'the Son of Man did not come to be served, but to serve, and give his life as a ransom for many' (Matt. 20:28). Jesus refused to call his disciples 'servants'. Instead, he called them 'friends' (John 15:15). And he said, 'greater love has no one than this – than to lay down his life for his friends' (John 15:13) – which he did. That's why I think it's probably more helpful to refer to 'the kingdom' as 'the kin(g)dom or 'kindom'. It's less about royalty and more about relationship and the way we ought to love one another.

Incarnating the Kingdom

In order to be to the change we want to see in the world, embodying 'heaven on earth', Jesus tells us we need live the attitudes he advocated in the Beatitudes. If we read the text carefully, we see that both the first and the last Beatitude are about experiencing 'the kingdom of heaven', or what I call 'the kindom of heaven'. And verse five seems to suggest those who 'inherit' heaven will do so on 'earth'.

> Blessed are the poor in spirit,
> for theirs is the kingdom of heaven.
> Blessed are those who mourn,
> for they will be comforted.
> Blessed are the meek,
> for they will inherit the earth.
> Blessed are those who hunger and thirst
> for righteousness,
> for they will be filled.
> Blessed are the merciful,
> for they will be shown mercy.
> Blessed are the pure in heart,
> for they will see God.

> Blessed are the peacemakers,
> for they will be called children of God.
> Blessed are those who are persecuted
> because of righteousness,
> for theirs is the kingdom of heaven.
> (Matthew 6:1-10)

In the beatitudes, the 'kingdom of heaven' is a place where the meek 'inherit the earth' (Matt.5.5); where those who give mercy will 'receive mercy' (Matt.5.7); where the hungry will be 'filled' (Luke 6.21) and those who hunger and thirst for justice will be 'fulfilled' (Matt.5.6). It is a place where those who mourn will be 'comforted' (Matt.5.4) and those who weep will now 'laugh' once more (Luke 6.21). It is a place where peacemakers will walk proudly as 'sons and daughters of God' (Matt.5.9) and all those who are pure in heart 'will see God' (Matt.5.8).

This 'kingdom of heaven on earth' - where people can see God face to face, live as God's children, be filled and fulfilled, find the comfort and the mercy that they need, wipe away their tears and have a smile that no one can wipe off their face - is the kind of place most of us hope and pray that our children and our children's children would inherit.

However, Jesus says we are faced with a choice: to be - or not to be - the change we want to see 'on earth as it is in heaven'. And in Luke's account of the Beatitudes, Jesus makes the choice - and its consequences for us - painfully clear.

Looking at his disciples, he said:
'Blessed are you who are poor,
for yours is the kingdom of God.
Blessed are you who hunger now,
for you will be satisfied.
Blessed are you who weep now,
for you will laugh.
Blessed are you when people hate you,
when they exclude you and insult you
and reject your name as evil,
because of the Son of Man.
Rejoice in that day and leap for joy,
because great is your reward in heaven.
For that is how their ancestors
treated the prophets.
But woe to you who are rich,
for you have already received your comfort.
Woe to you who are well fed now,
for you will go hungry.
Woe to you who laugh now,
for you will mourn and weep.
Woe to you when all people speak well of you,
for that is how their ancestors
treated the false prophets.'
(Luke 6:20-26)

In Luke's account of the Beatitudes here Jesus is using classic Jewish parallelism to compare and contrast two completely different positive and negative scenarios.

Positive Scenario	Negative Scenario
Blessed are the poor (and those with the poor in spirit) for yours is the kingdom of God.	But woe to you who are rich, (and all those into status and success) for you have received your comfort.
Blessed are you who hunger now, for you will be satisfied.	(But) woe to you who are well fed now, for you will go hungry.
Blessed are you who weep now, for you will laugh.	(But) woe to you who laugh now, for you will . . . weep.
Blessed are you when people hate you . . . because of the Son of Man, for that is how their ancestors treated the (true) prophets.	(But) woe to you when all people speak well of you, for that is how their ancestors treated the false prophets

So Jesus is saying that we need to think about the consequences of our choices.

Either we can . . .	Or we can . . .
Be poor *(or be with the poor in spirit)* And we will be blessed for the kingdom of God is ours.	**Be rich** *(and be into status and success)* And we will be cursed because we put our trust in riches.
Be hungry *(and hunger for justice)* And we will be blessed for God will satisfy our hunger.	**Be comfy** *(and be well-off and well-fed)* And we will be cursed for nothing will satisfy us.

Either we can . . .	Or we can . . .
Be sad *(weeping with those who weep)* And we will be blessed for we will have the last laugh.	**Be happy** *(laughing with those who laugh)* And we will be cursed for we will regret not really caring.
Be unpopular *(and get bad press because of our commitment to Christ)* And we will be blessed because we are part of a great tradition of courageous integrity.	**Be popular** *(and get good press because we collude with the status quo)* And we will be cursed because we will have gained celebrity but lost our integrity in the process.

Let's be frank. On first hearing, the call to be poor, hungry, sad, and unpopular is not an attractive option, is it? It's exactly the opposite of what most of us aspire to. But on second hearing, this call – to be poor and to be with the poor in spirit, to be hungry and to be hungry for justice, to be sad because we are weeping with those that weep, and to be unpopular because we are committed to following the way of Christ with integrity – is quite intriguing, quite challenging, quite exciting.

And the more we think about it, the more we begin to slowly but surely realize that the call to be with the poor in spirit, to be hungry for justice, to be sad because we are weeping with those that weep, and to be unpopular because we are committed to following the way of Christ with integrity, is in fact the only way that the kingdom of God can be ours. It's the only way that God can satisfy our hunger for justice, and it's the only way that we can have the last laugh as part of that great tradition of people with integrity who suffered scorn but triumphed at the end.

As Brian McLaren says, 'The kingdom of heaven comes to people who crave not victory but justice, who seek not revenge but mercy, who strive for peace and who are courageously eager to suffer pain for the cause of justice, not inflict it'.[6] And in the light of that knowledge we know we need to make a choice: to be – or not to be – the change we want to see.

If we want to be the change we want to see in the world, we need to remember what Jesus says in Matthew's account. We need to be:

Poor – and identify with the poor in spirit	
Empathic – and grieve over the injustice in the world	
Meek – and get angry about injustice, but not aggressive	
Hungry and thirsty for righteousness – and seek for justice	
Merciful – and extend compassion to all those in need	
Pure in heart – and wholehearted in our desire to do right	
Peacemakers – and work for peace in a world that's at war	
Persecuted for righteousness – and suffer for just causes	

Imagine what would happen if we chose to be the change we want to see in the world and adopted these Be-Attitudes in order to embody the kingdom of heaven on earth . . .

We'd identify with the poor in spirit.
We'd grieve over injustice in the world.
We'd get angry, but never aggressive.
We'd seek to do justice, even to our enemies.

We'd extend compassion to all those in need.

We'd act with integrity, not just for the publicity.

We'd work for peace in the midst of the violence.

We'd suffer ourselves, rather than inflict suffering.[7]

The Good Samaritan

Of all the tales Jesus tells, there is no better example of what it looks like to embody these Be-Attitudes than the story of the man we know as the Good Samaritan.

> On one occasion an expert in the law stood up to test Jesus. 'Teacher,' he asked, 'what must I do to inherit eternal life?' 'What is written in the Law?' he replied. 'How do you read it?'
>
> He answered: '"Love the Lord your God with all your heart and with all your soul and with all your strength and with all your mind"; and, "Love your neighbour as yourself."' 'You have answered correctly,' Jesus replied. 'Do this and you will live.' But he wanted to justify himself, so he asked Jesus, 'And who is my neighbour?' In reply Jesus said: 'A man was going down from Jerusalem to Jericho, when he fell into the hands of robbers. They stripped him of his clothes, beat him and went away, leaving him half dead. A priest happened to be going down the same road, and when he saw the man, he passed by on the other side. So too, a Levite, when he came to the place and saw him, passed by on the other side. But a

Samaritan, as he travelled, came where the man
was; and when he saw him, he took pity on him.
He went to him and bandaged his wounds,
pouring on oil and wine. Then he put the man on
his own donkey, took him to an inn and took care
of him. The next day he took out two silver coins
and gave them to the innkeeper. "Look after him,"
he said, "and when I return, I will reimburse you
for any extra expense you may have." Which of
these three do you think was a neighbour to the
man who fell into the hands of robbers?' The
expert in the law replied, 'The one who had mercy
on him.' Jesus told him, 'Go and do likewise.'
(Luke 10:25-37)

Now what would you say is the point of this story? I can
think of three points.

1. The first point would be that we need to show mercy to
   others. (Yes. But there is more)

2. The second point would be that we need to show mercy
   to those who are not the same as we are. (Yes. But if that
   was the only other point that Jesus wanted to make, the
   rescuer in the story would have been a Jew and the
   victim in the story would have been a Samaritan).

3. The third - and most important - point that Jesus
   wanted to make in this story (by casting the Jew in the
   role of the victim and the Samaritan in the role of the
   rescuer) is that sometimes the only way we learn about
   the need to show mercy to those who are different from

us is if we learn this from a righteous person from a different religion.

When we read the story of the Good Samaritan in light of the Be-Attitudes that we've discussed it's clear that, on the one hand, Jesus was condemning the leaders of his own religion for not practicing what he preached. And, on the other hand, we see that Jesus was commending a despised person from a different religion as a great example of all that Jesus was trying to teach them.

The Good Samaritan embodied the Be-Attitudes perfectly. He identified with the '*poor man*' he came across '*in spirit*'. He '*grieved*' over the injustice done him like he '*grieved*' over the injustice done to himself. He got '*angry enough to act*', but controlled his rage so he used his energy constructively to deal with the injustice. He '*sought to do justice*' to the victim, by rescuing him from danger, even though the Jew was the Samaritan's traditional enemy. He '*extended mercy*' to the broken man, by bathing his wounds in oil, binding his injuries in cloth, carrying him to safety on his donkey, and not only paying for his care at a road side inn, but also offering to pay more, if what he had already paid was not enough. He '*acted with integrity*', not for the publicity, by quietly helping the man, and then quickly moving on. In so doing he '*built a bridge of peace*' between the Samaritans and the Jews '*at the risk of being ridiculed by both sides*'. In other words, *the Good Samaritan embodied the Be-Attitudes celebrated in the Beatitudes.*

And Jesus says to all who would listen, 'Go and do likewise' (Luke 10:25-37).

Who do you think Jesus would cast as the Good Samaritan if he were telling the story to Christians today? I have no doubt he would give the role to someone who Christians despise as much as Samaritans were despised by Jews. There are many possibilities. I think it would depend on the particular prejudices of the Christian to whom he was speaking. But my guess is there would be a good chance that Jesus would choose a Good Muslim for the role of the Good Samaritan.

Let me tell you about three Good Muslims I know who are great examples to me.[8]

I met Hasan as a Hazara asylum seeker. He is a doctor who had to flee Afghanistan after the fall of the Taliban for treating Pushtu soldiers who were wounded in an attack on his village. Hasan now has his resident visa and serves the refugee community as their mental health worker, helping them cope with their painful experiences of torture and trauma. I once asked Hasan how his faith in God affected his community work and he said, 'Allah is merciful and we should be merciful too.'

Rahim is Hasan's friend. I met him when I met Hasan. He is an agriculturalist who had to flee Afghanistan when his development work for the United Nations made him a marked man. He bumped into Hasan when they jumped onto the same leaky boat that was heading to Australia. Since he has arrived, Rahim has worked with my son-in-law Marty in setting up a co-op to provide work for unemployed refugees. Many times Rahim has been offered easier work with higher pay. But he has consistently rejected better options for himself to create better options for others.

Asif owns the café across the road. He is a dedicated Muslim who migrated from Indonesia to Australia many years ago. Asif recently decided to be initiated as a dervish in the Sufi tradition. I have been meeting regularly with Asif for some time now to encourage each other in our faith. Asif reckons that the best thing that people from the Abrahamic traditions can do - to nurture a spirited faith, over against our doctrinaire beliefs - is to recover the radical compassion of Jesus. Time and again it is the gentle voice of my Sufi friend who calls me back to the example of Jesus. Only last week, we spent an hour together meditating on the love of God revealed to us in Jesus.

Jesus says to all who would listen: 'Go and do likewise' (Luke 10:25-37).

The Holy Spirit

My Muslim friend Asif is right when he says we that need to nurture a 'spirited faith' rather than 'doctrinaire beliefs' if we are ever going to recover the radical compassion of Jesus and practice Jesus' Be-Attitudes like the Good Samaritan.

Jesus said there is always a mystery about the way the Spirit breathes vitality into our lives. Sometimes it comes screaming into our lives like a storm in a gale, rattling through the valley of dry bones at the bottom of our souls. However, probably most times it comes with a whisper on a zephyr of wind that gusts so gently we scarcely notice it speaking a still small word into our subconscious minds.

Jesus said no one really knows how or when or where it will come. He said, 'The wind blows wherever it pleases.

You hear its sound, but you cannot tell where it comes from or where it is going' (John 3:8). Jesus also said that the one thing that is necessary is to be open to it when it does come – so we can make the most of the opportunity we have to be 'born again of the Spirit' (John 3:8).

Jesus told his disciples about the role of the Spirit in his life. He said it was not duty, or obligation, or rules and regulations, but rather the Spirit who was at the heart of the Be-Attitudes he embodied (Luke 4:18). He set the disciples an example of how to practice the Be-Attitudes, and he encouraged them to practice the Be-Attitudes themselves. But he also made it clear that unless they were energized by the Spirit there was just no way they would be able to sustain the life of radical, non-violent, sacrificial compassion that the Be-Attitudes required. So, not surprisingly, the last thing Jesus told his disciples before he left was not to go anywhere until they were 'filled with the Spirit'. He said that, sooner or later, the day would come when they would all be 'immersed' in the Spirit. And if they were empty and open and receptive, he told them, and created a hospitable space in their hearts, then when they were 'immersed' in the Spirit they would naturally be filled in the Spirit (Acts 1:4).

• • •

In order to create a hospitable space in their hearts for the Spirit, the disciples spent time together 'constantly in prayer' (Acts 1:14). For the disciples, prayer was a process of developing an awareness of, and an availability to, the Spirit. It involved waiting upon the Spirit and a willingness to yield to the Spirit. It was essentially a desire to live life wholly and solely in the *joie de vivre* of the Spirit. Prayer had an important place in their life together, because they recognized that the *joie de vivre* of the Spirit was the centre of energy that they needed to practice the Be-Attitudes.

Prayer became the 'still point' around which their lives revolved. It was the 'point of integration' where their inner and outer conflicts were resolved. It was the 'starting point' at which people began to live again, as well as the 'point of departure' from which people began to experiment with practicing the Be-Attitudes (Acts 1:12–26).

The disciples prayed constantly because, finally, after trying and failing to do it themselves, they came to realize that it was only in encounter with the Spirit that all that was good could be affirmed, and all that was evil could be confronted. Only with the Spirit could they outline their task for the future, glimpse a vision of justice, and realize an infusion of grace. Only in the Spirit could they access the vitality they needed to practice the Be-Attitudes and engage in the struggle for the salvation of the world.

• • •

When the Spirit came at Pentecost the disciples were ready. Nonetheless, it was still a completely unexpected, surprising, wild, and wonderful ride . . .

> When the day of Pentecost came, they were all together in one place. Suddenly a sound like the blowing of a violent wind came from heaven and filled the whole house where they were sitting.

They saw what seemed to be tongues of fire that separated and came to rest on each of them. All of them were filled with the Holy Spirit and began to speak in other tongues as the Spirit enabled them. Now there were staying in Jerusalem God-fearing Jews from every nation under heaven. When they heard this sound, a crowd came together in bewilderment . . . Amazed and perplexed, they asked one another, 'What does this mean?' Some, however, made fun of them and said, 'They have had too much wine.' Then Peter stood up with the Eleven, raised his voice and addressed the crowd: 'Fellow Jews and all of you who live in Jerusalem, let me explain this to you; listen carefully to what I say. These people are not drunk, as you suppose. It's only nine in the morning! No, this is what was spoken by the prophet Joel: 'In the last days, God says, I will pour out my Spirit on all people.' (Acts 2:1-18)

I think we can identify with both kinds of reactions to this event. We might start out saying to ourselves, 'These people are out of their minds!' But we would probably end up asking ourselves the big question: 'What does all this mean?' I think this event means many things.

The activity of the Spirit is always anonymous. We hear the wind, look around to see who is there and, on an occasion such as this, see 'tongues of fire', but on most other occasions we probably see nothing at all. But even when there are 'tongues of fire' they act as signs that point to otherwise singularly unimportant people – most of whose names we do not know and never do get to know – as the centre of attention on this particular occasion. The apostle Paul says that this is typical of the self-effacing way the Spirit works – anonymously empowering ordinary people to do extraordinary things. In writing to the faith community at Corinth Paul says,

> Brothers and sisters, think of what you were when you were called. Not many of you were wise by human standards; not many were influential; not many were of noble birth. But God chose the foolish things of the world to shame the wise; God chose the weak things of the world to shame the strong. God chose the lowly things of this world –and the things that are not – to nullify the things that are. (1 Cor. 1:26-28)

The apostle Peter says that ordinary people need no longer be subject to the prophets, priests, and kings who traditionally ruled their lives because, through the power of the Spirit, they have become 'A chosen people, a royal priesthood, a holy nation' (1 Pet. 2:9). Now, as prophetic people, they can bear witness to God's agenda of love and justice for the world; as priestly people they can intercede for those in need themselves; and as royal people they can actually anticipate and represent the kingdom of heaven on earth.[9]

The 'tongues of fire' are symbolic of the way the Spirit takes 'nobodies', like these poor despised, uneducated Galileans, and makes them 'somebodies'. Fire has always been an archetypal image of passion. It's common for us to say that someone 'burns with desire'. The Spirit came at Pentecost and put people in touch with their passion. The Spirit doesn't put people in touch with an abstract ideal but with the reality of their true selves. The Spirit relates to each person individually and fills the hospitable space in the heart he or she has created with a burning desire to become the person that God has created him or her to be - the person that deep down he or she really wants to be. Paul talks about the powers of the Spirit as 'the energies for a new life' (1 Cor. 12:6, 11). 'They are gifts of grace [and] the gifts of grace (*charismata*) lead to ready, courteous service (*diakonia*). Through the powers of the Spirit, the one Spirit gives every individual [a] specific calling, what is exactly cut out for [them], in the process of the new creation.'[10]

The text states that tongues of fire came to 'rest' on each person as if the fire sat with each of them comfortably, burning brightly but not dangerously, generating more light than heat. The implication here is that when someone yields to the burning desire to become the person that God created him or her to be, it will not lead to 'burnout'. Burnout comes not from being 'too fired up', but from being fired up about an abstract ideal of ourselves - rather than the reality of who we are meant to be. Community worker Parker Palmer writes from painful personal experience: 'Burnout does not come from giving too much, but from trying to give what we do not have to begin with.'[11] He says that 'the liberation of society comes not from those who try to change society, but from those who try to be their true selves'.[12] Indeed, he says the sustainable spiritual dynamic for liberation takes place at the intersection of where our true selves engage the real world around about us.[13]

Pentecost shows us that when we are filled with a burning desire to engage the real world in the light of our true selves, we're able to relate to the world with a much greater degree of sensitivity. While most people are willing to give intellectual assent to the importance of greater sensitivity, we cannot achieve this sensitivity unless we give emotional affirmation to that intellectual assent in our hearts - just as the Spirit inspires. The issue is not so much a conflict between our heads and our hearts as it is a conflict within our hearts. In our hearts we know that we cannot live without love, and that love involves an enhanced 'sensibility' - an enhanced appreciation of, and affection for, one another's lives. But in our hearts we also know that if we develop this enhanced sensibility towards the beautiful, yet painful, reality of one another's lives it will inevitably entail great agony as well as great joy.[14]

So we vacillate between wanting to become more loving and wanting to become anything but more loving. As we prevaricate we are tempted to withdraw from sensibility, which involves a greater sensitivity towards the total reality of one another's lives, into sentimentality, which involves more sensitivity to those parts of one another's lives which are less painful (like rumour, innuendo, scandal, and trivia) and less sensitivity to those parts of one another's lives that are more painful (like disadvantage, disability, disease, and death).[15] Thus we tend to retreat into an unreal world of infotainment, sitcoms, chat shows, and 'hot gos' magazines that give us the illusion of relating to the real world – all while we are not relating to the real world at all.

However, the only way we can live is to live in the real world. And the only way we can live in the real world is to love the real world. And the only way we can love the real world is by overcoming our fear of the suffering that love in the real world involves. And the only way we can overcome our fear of suffering is to be filled by the Spirit with a burning desire to love the world. This desire from the Spirit is so passionate that we can risk the pain in the world in order to embrace the world – and love it as it is.[16] And that is what the Be-Attitudes are all about.

• • •

When the Spirit came at Pentecost, people began to practice the Be-Attitudes to such an extent they were able to create an exceptionally inclusive, completely egalitarian, post-Pentecost community.

> They devoted themselves to the apostles' teaching and to the fellowship, to the breaking of bread and to prayer. Everyone was filled with awe, and many wonders and miraculous signs were done by the apostles. All the believers were together and had everything in common. Selling their possessions and goods, they gave to anyone as they had need. Every day they continued to meet together in the

temple courts. They broke bread in their homes and ate together with glad and sincere hearts, praising God and enjoying the favour of all the people. And the Lord added to their number daily those who were being saved. (Acts 2:42-47)

All the believers were one in heart and mind. No one claimed any of their possessions was their own, but they shared everything they had. With great power the apostles testified to the resurrection of the Lord Jesus, and much grace was upon them all. There were no needy persons among them. For from time to time those who owned lands or houses sold them, brought the money from the sales and put it at the apostles' feet, and it was distributed to anyone as he had need. (Acts 4:32-35)

This is an not an exclusive 'Christian' community but an inclusive 'Christ-like' community - committed to the way of Christ as a way of relating respectfully to all people regardless of religion, tradition, status, class, caste, age, or gender. It creates a society - albeit partially and temporarily - in which the grace of God is the order of the day. The people 'have everything in common', they 'distribute their resources to anyone according to their need' and, consequently, there is no one with an unmet need - 'no needy persons among them'! This is an extraordinarily beautiful manifestation of the kingdom of heaven on earth.

• • •

Since Pentecost, whenever people have opened themselves to the Spirit like the disciples did they have found themselves being inspired to be able to engage reality, make responsible choices, and take compassionate action. For example:

> A woman in a London flat was told of her husband's death in a street accident. The shock of grief stunned her like a blow, she sank into a corner of the sofa and sat there rigid and unhearing. For a long time her terrible tranced look continued to embarrass the family . . . Then the schoolteacher of one of her children . . . called . . . and sat down beside her. Without a word she threw an arm around the tight shoulders, clasping them with her full strength. [One cheek touched the other.] Then as the unrelenting pain seeped through to her the newcomer's tears began to flow, falling on their two hands . . . For a long time that is all that was happening. And then at last the [widow] began to sob. Still not a word was spoken and after a little while the visitor got up and went.[17]

Bishop John Taylor says that 'the Holy Spirit is the force in the straining muscles of an arm, the film of sweat between pressed cheeks, the mingled wetness of the backs of clasped hands'[18] that enables us to practice the Be-Attitudes.

Part Two

The Kingdom Can Come On Earth

– Through Us

When Jesus shared with his disciples the passion he had to be the change he wanted to see in the world, he said to them, 'this is how you ought to pray':

> Our Father in heaven,
> hallowed be your name,
> your kingdom come,
> your will be done
> on earth as it is in heaven.
> Give us today our daily bread.
> Forgive us our debts,
> as we also have forgiven our debtors.
> And lead us not into temptation,
> but deliver us from evil.
> (Matt. 6:9-13)

• • •

Jesus does not talk to God as 'Yahweh' or 'Adonai' but as 'Abba' - or 'Papa'. Some of us who have been abused by an earthly father might find it easier to relate to God as our heavenly 'Mama' rather than our heavenly 'Papa'. Whatever our term of endearment might be, Jesus invites us to relate to God as a committed, caring, kindly, protective, nurturing, loving cosmic parent.

As we have seen, Judeo-Christian faith involves 'deep trust in the watchful love of God for all God's children. According to the prophet Isaiah, even in the midst of the most terrible circumstances, those whose hearts are centred in God's faithful care "shall renew their strength, they shall mount up on wings like eagles, they shall run and not be weary, they shall walk and not faint".[19]

David Benner reminds us that 'while human love can never bear the weight of our need for divine love, it can teach us about divine love. Human love can communicate divine love. Experiences of human love make the idea of God's love believable. The relative constancy of the love of family and friends makes the absolute faithfulness of divine love at least conceivable.' However, Benner reiterates again and again that there is 'no substitute for learning what love really is by coming back to the source. God's love is the original that shows up the limitations of all copies. Only God's love is capable of making us into great lovers.'[20]

Wayne Muller says that 'it is not the fact of being loved that is life changing. It is the experience of allowing [ourselves] to be loved'.[21] This experiential knowledge of ourselves as deeply loved by God deepens our thoughts with new data about our world and deepens our feelings with new attitudes towards our world. In the light of our knowledge of God's love we know we can trust God – and so we can take risks and courageously embrace the world in which we live.

> God's love connects us to all of God's creation and all of God's creatures. It moves us 'from the isolation of self-interest to a connection with life that cannot allow any ultimate divisions. It does not allow [us] to limit [our] interest to those within [our] tribe – whether those tribal boundaries are understood in religious, ethnic or national terms'. Instead it involves us in a 'movement beyond the hardened boundaries of the isolated self to the selves-in-relationship that make up community' leading to 'a sense of [our] oneness with all' life.[22]

If we all relate to God as our parent, that makes us all siblings, sharing the intrinsic connections that brothers and sisters have with one another. Few of us have understood the implications of these connections as deeply as Desmond Tutu has. He says, 'God's dream is that all of us will realize that we are family, that we are made for togetherness. In God's family, there are no outsiders, no enemies. Black and white, rich and poor, gay and straight, Jew and Arab, Muslim and Christian, Hindu and Buddhist – all belong.' Tutu says that 'God's love is too great to be confined to any one side of a conflict or to any one religion. People are shocked when I say that George Bush and Saddam Hussein are brothers, that Yasser Arafat and Ariel Sharon are brothers, but God says, "All are my children." It is shocking. But it is true.' Further, he says, 'this dream can be found throughout the Bible . . . love is universal. You don't have to believe in God to know that loving is better than hating. When we start to live [in love], as brothers and sisters, and to recognize our interdependence, we become fully human.'[23]

A 'New Dark Age'

The core request Jesus makes to God in his prayer is 'hallowed be your name'. The word 'hallow' means 'to make holy'. The request for God's name to 'be hallowed', or 'to be made holy', implies that right now God's name is not being hallowed, not being treated as holy, and that we – as the people of God – are invited to restore God's reputation on the planet. The truth is that God has a bad reputation because bad things are going down in God's world. I'm not alone in thinking that we are moving into a 'New Dark Age'. Jacques Attali, who was a professor of economics at l'École Polytechnique in Paris and who was appointed as the first president of the European Bank for Reconstruction and Development, based in London, says:

> By 2050, 8 billion people will populate the earth. More than two-thirds will live in the poorest countries. Seeking to escape their desperate fate, millions will attempt to leave behind their misery to seek a decent life elsewhere. But neither the Pacific nor the European spheres will accept the majority of poor nomads. They will close their borders to immigrants. Quotas will be erected and restrictions imposed. [Renewed] social norms will ostracize foreigners. Like the fortified cities of the Middle Ages, the centres of privilege will construct barriers of all kinds, trying to protect their wealth.[24]

As I look around, I can see signs that the 'New Dark Age' has begun. Some of the features of emerging neo-feudalism that I observe include:

1. The emergence of powerful, unelected and/or unaccountable leaders.

2. These 'lords' offering protection in return for subservience and services.

3. People are given a choice – they can be either 'for' or 'against' these 'lords'.

4. The people who are 'for' these 'lords' live their lives as their 'vassals'.

5. 'Vassals' wait on these 'lords', live off the crumbs that fall from their lords' tables, and find refuge – in times of danger – inside their lords' 'castles'.

6. The people who are 'against' these 'lords' are branded as 'infidels'.

7. The 'lords' wipe out 'infidels' – by leaving them to starve 'outside their gates' in times of hunger or by slaughtering them in 'crusades'.

8. There are no universal basic human rights. The only 'right' is 'might'.

9. 'Civilization' is the private preserve of these 'lords' and their 'vassals'.

10. And they justify this iniquitous 'civilization' in the name of religion!

Zbigniew Brzezinski, who served as United States National Security Advisor in the Carter Administration, supervised the beginning of the Afghan war and credits himself for having brought down the Soviet system. In the true spirit of the son of a Polish aristocrat he says: 'The three imperatives of geopolitical strategy are to maintain security dependence among the vassals, keep tributaries pliant, and keep the barbarians from coming together.'[25]

Australian sociologist Ghassan Hage says that 'not so long ago the state was committed to the welfare of everyone within its borders. We even called it "the welfare state".

That is no longer so.'[26] 'We seem to be reverting to neo-feudal times, when the boundaries of civilisation no longer coincide with the boundaries of the nation, but the boundaries of upper class society.'[27] Hage says that 'there are no universal rights – only the privilege of the elite'.[28] Further, he says, 'we are increasingly witnessing the rise of a culture that combines a siege [castle] and warring [crusade] mentality; by necessity it emphasizes the exclusion [and/or] eradication of the potentially threatening other'.[29] He says that 'in each country now – there are first-world elites and third-world threats to the elites. In this neo-feudal age the challenge is not how to integrate the marginalised but how to rid ourselves of these third-world [threats] – not just the terrorists, but the refugees and refugee claimants we have on our doorstep.'[30]

We are beginning to build more and more of what we euphemistically call 'gated communities'. These are citadels guarded by walls, infra-red cameras, heat-sensitive alarms, and private security companies. They are purpose-built – as the developer of Sanctuary Cove put it – 'to keep the [human] cockroaches out!' And there is some evidence to indicate that the previous government tried to turn the whole continent of Australia into a 'gated community' like Sanctuary Cove. Millions of dollars of government funds – dollars that were supposed to have been dedicated to foreign aid – have been spent on what the previous government called its 'Pacific Solution' – a flotilla of heavily-armed patrols dedicated to preventing asylum seekers from ever setting foot upon our shores. It is a policy that is neither 'pacific' nor a 'solution'. It was simply meant 'to keep the "illegal" "queue-jumping" cockroaches out!'

Inside the walls of our well-protected pleasure dome we enjoy lives of unparalleled luxury. As part of the top twenty per cent of the world's population, we have more than eighty per cent of the world's total income. In the last decade of the last century more of us became millionaires than during any decade in history. And when it comes to our comparative level of income, we are so well-off by world standards that even those at the bottom of our economic ladder who are living on social security are still in the top twenty per cent of the global population – with incomparable access to world-class social, educational, and medical services.

Outside the ramparts of these fortresses of safety and security, others are condemned en masse to an existence characterized by cycles of increasing degrees of deprivation and violence. The bottom twenty per cent of the world's population try to survive on less than one and a half per cent of the world's income. So more than twenty-five thousand people die every day of every week of every year – simply because they cannot access their fair share of the world's income. In desperation, many sell their labour for a pittance. More than two hundred and fifty million children work for as little as twenty-five cents a day. As a last resort, many even have to sell their bodies. More than a million children are forced into prostitution every year. Millions of kids under the age of fifteen are developing HIV and dying of AIDS. Life is, literally, 'hell on earth'.

More than one hundred and twenty million people were killed in wars during the twentieth century. Currently more than twenty million people are fleeing from carnage and ruin. Some beg for entry to our country – but in Australia we take less than five thousand a year. Some beg for charity – but apart from giving generously towards relief from the occasional spectacular disaster on our doorstep – like the recent tsunami appeal – Aussies give on average less than five dollar a year.

And where is God in all this? Well, if you believe two of the most famous 'God-fearing leaders' of our times, God is only making things go from bad to worse. On September 11, 2001, Osama Bin Laden ordered an attack on the twin towers of the World Trade Center at the heart of the American empire. As the world looked on in astonishment Bin Laden cried, 'Here is America struck by God Almighty in one of its vital organs, so that its greatest buildings are destroyed.'[31] In retaliation, George W. Bush ordered an attack on Osama Bin Laden in Afghanistan – and also an attack on Saddam Hussein in Iraq (who did not have any weapons of mass destruction, or anything to do with the 9-11 attack, but who had tried to kill George Bush, Sr). Bush claimed that 'God told me to strike al-Qaeda and I struck them, and then he instructed me to strike at Saddam, which I did'.[32] God's got a bad reputation because God gets blamed for the violence on both sides.

In spite of what Osama Bin Laden and George W. Bush might say, Jesus' prayer protests loudly that God's will is not being done on earth as it is in heaven. In fact, Jesus' prayer insists that God's damaged reputation will only ever be able to be truly restored when God's will is really 'done on earth – as it is in heaven'.

• • •

Jesus' prayer suggests that anyone who is passionate about doing God's will on earth as it is in heaven will be passionate about feeding the hungry – and forgiving debts – and thereby freeing all the debt-slaves from their bondage.

Jesus doesn't teach his disciples to pray: 'give me this day my daily bread'. Jesus teaches his disciples to pray: 'give us this day our daily bread'. Through his prayer, Jesus invites his disciples to make his passion – for every man, woman, and child in the world to have their basic needs met – their own. John says, 'This is how we know what love is: Jesus Christ laid down his life for us. And we ought to lay down our lives for our brothers and sisters. If any of us has material possessions and sees a brother or sister in need but has no pity on them, how can the love of God be in us? Dear children, let us not love with words or in speech, but with deeds and in truth' (1 John 3:16-17).

Jesus teaches his disciples to pray 'forgive us our debts as we have forgiven our debtors'. Note that the word Jesus uses here is not 'sin' but, literally, 'debt'. What Jesus says that is so important about forgiveness is not that we preach it, but that we practice it. There is no liberation from the cycles of poverty in our lives without forgiveness. And we have no right to expect forgiveness if we do not extend forgiveness. We need to develop a global culture of forgiveness. Jesus says, 'For if you forgive people when they sin against you, your heavenly Father will also forgive you. But if you do not forgive people their sins, your Father will not forgive your sins' (Matt. 6:14-15). Note that the word Jesus uses here is not 'debt' but 'sin'. He seems to be saying that in order to show God's love in the world we should start by forgiving cash 'debts' and move on to forgiving all kinds of 'debts' – or 'sins', if you like. In this way we can be liberated not only from our cycles of poverty, but also from our cycles of violence.

Jesus says, 'You have heard that it was said, "Love your neighbour and hate your enemy." But I tell you: Love your enemies and pray for those who persecute you, that you may be children of your Father in heaven. He causes his sun to rise on the evil and the good, and sends rain on the righteous and the unrighteous. Be perfect as your heavenly Father is perfect' (Matt. 5:43-48). He says to us, 'Let your light shine before people' in this 'New Dark Age', 'that they may see your good deeds' – not your good ideas, or your good intentions, but your good deeds – and so 'have a reason to praise your Father who is in heaven'. At long last, then, they can glimpse something of the goodness of God at work in their world in the way that you live your life (Matt. 5:16).

Brother Suns and Sister Moons

In my view, the only hope for a world entering a 'New Dark Age' is the emergence of new movements of Brother Suns and Sister Moons. The story of 'Brother Sun and Sister Moon' was first told in the twelfth-century Dark Age in Italy.

Francis was born to a French mother and Italian father in 1182, and his father called him Francesco – or Francis – after a trip to France. The 'little Frenchman' was brought up on romantic French ballads sung by travelling troubadours. The son of a wealthy merchant, Francis led a cavalier life in his youth and was considered 'the life of the party' by his contemporaries. Francis' dream was to one day become a knight. So when he was in his early twenties, Francis took the opportunity to fight for Assisi against a neighbouring town. Young Francis' haughty military career came to an abrupt halt, however, when he was captured and incarcerated. This experience was to prove a turning point for Francis. During his year in prison and the year in convalescence following his release, Francis thought long and hard about his life. His dream of becoming a knight seemed ridiculous in the light of the harsh reality of war that had confronted him. One day when he was riding along a road he simply stopped dead in his tracks. It was as if he simply could not carry on anymore as he was. He dismounted, undressed, then bit by bit he took all his knightly regalia – including his horse, his sword, and his armour – and gave it all away.

His father became exasperated with Francis over his prodigality with the family's property and organized a meeting with the local bishop to pull him into line – but that plan backfired. Francis responded to his father's complaints by renouncing his family, and his family's property, altogether. Right there and then he gave back everything his family had given him, including the clothes that he was wearing at the time. Francis stood there, naked as the day he was born, and turned to his father and said, 'Until now I have called you father, but from now on I can say without reserve, "Our Father who is in Heaven" - He is all my wealth - I place my confidence in Him.'

In order to consider his future, Francis decided to spend some time living as a hermit beside an old church in San Damiano. While he was there Francis heard a voice calling him, saying, 'Rebuild my church.' Francis responded to the call by repairing the ruins of the church in San Damiano and then set about the task of reforming the life of the church throughout Italy. Francis approached the task of renewal not as a legislator but as a juggler. Troubadours, singing romantic ballads that stirred the heart, often came to his house while he was growing up. He aspired to be like one of the jugglers who accompanied the troubadours, drawing the crowds for the musicians so they could listen to the music of the heart that they played. As *Le Jongleur de Dieu,* a 'Juggler for God', Francis wanted to travel from town to town like an entertainer, without a penny to his name, introducing people to *joie de vivre* - the 'true joy of living'.

Considering his views, it is quite remarkable that Francis did not rage against the pompous opulence of medieval society. Instead, ever the romantic, Francis tried to woo the people away from their preoccupation with the trappings of power so they could fall in love with the lovely 'Lady Poverty'. Poverty was not an end in itself. But, as far as

Francis was concerned, people needed to be willing to joyfully embrace poverty in order to practice the Be-Attitudes and joyfully embrace the poor.

In 1210 Francis obtained approval for a simple rule dedicated to 'apostolic poverty'. He called the order the 'Friars Minor' and this band of 'Little Brothers' followed the example of their founder in caring for the poor. Then in 1212 Clare, a wealthy friend from Assisi who, like Francis, had been converted and had given all her wealth to the poor, started a sister order to the brothers that was to become known as 'the Poor Clares'.

Francis and Clare set about their task with such enthusiasm that people wanted to join them. And, as hundreds and thousands of people from all over Europe joined them, the humble movement of 'Brother Sun and Sister Moon' began to gradually engage and eventually change the Dark Age in which they lived – in the light of the gospel.

Pope Urban II had called for a 'crusade', or 'Holy War', to be led by 'Christian Knights' who would take up arms and sally forth to fight against 'the enemies of Christ'. 'Cursed be the man who holds back his sword from shedding blood!' was the blood-curdling cry of Pope Gregory VII ringing in the ears of the 'soldier of Christ'. And so away they went. Over the course of the next two centuries, Christians threw themselves into the task of killing thousands, if not millions, of 'heretics' and 'heathens'. The People's Crusade sacked Belgrade which, next to Constantinople, was the greatest non-Catholic Orthodox city in the world. In 1204, the crusaders attacked

Constantinople. They raped, pillaged, and plundered this great Christian city, without mercy, in the name of Christ.

In the meantime, the crusaders also managed to assault the Holy City of Jerusalem and to slaughter its Jewish and Muslim inhabitants. Raymond of Aguilers enthusiastically eulogized the massacre as 'a just and marvellous judgement of God':

> Numbers of Saracens were beheaded. Others were shot with arrows, or forced to jump from towers; others were tortured for several days, they burned with flames. In the streets were seen piles of heads and hands and feet. One rode about everywhere amid the corpses of men and horses. The horses waded in blood up to their knees, nay, up to their bridle. It was a just and marvellous judgement of God, that this place should be filled with the blood of unbelievers![33]

Francis refused point-blank to take up arms himself. And he managed to persuade his followers not to carry weapons under any circumstances – even for the purpose of self-defence. He made his way to Egypt, where the crusaders were fighting, and went about the camps begging them to remember the words of Christ – 'that those who live by the sword will die by the sword' – and beseeching them all to lay down their arms. When they refused to listen to him, Francis crossed the lines at Damietta and went to talk with the 'enemy' sultan Mele-el-Khamil – to tell him about his beloved 'Prince of Peace' and to try to broker a peace deal 'in His name'.

Many historians consider the rule of life that Francis and Clare advocated for lay people to be one of the major factors in the demise of the feudalism that defined the Dark Age of their day. Francis and Clare were concerned by the very sophisticated and effective system of control (upon which our postmodern system of oppression and exploitation may well be based), built as it was on the foundation of a network of castles guarded by towering walls and protected by heavily-armed patrols of freelance mercenaries. And they undermined this system simply by encouraging their brothers and sisters to practice the Be-Attitudes – to lay aside their weapons, to unlock the gates of the castles, to welcome outsiders in, and to share their wealth gladly with the poor.

• • •

A classic example of the impact of their movement that is relevant to us is the life of Elisabeth von Thuringia, known as the 'Elisabeth of Many Castles'. Elisabeth was born in 1207, probably at Pressburg, in Thuringia. She was the daughter of King Andrew II and Queen Gertrude of Hungary. King Andrew II was, by all reports, a bad king whose misrule led his nobles to lead a revolt against him. They eventually managed to get the king to sign an edict called the Golden Bull, a charter of rights and responsibilities which was Hungary's version of the Magna Carta. Queen Gertrude was apparently a good woman who, unfortunately, was implicated in the politics of the day and was assassinated by the nobles in 1213. Elisabeth was just seven years old when her mother was murdered.

But before she died Gertrude managed to do two things that were to shape the rest of her daughter's life. The first was to share her faith with her daughter. Gertrude was a devout Christian, and she encouraged Elisabeth from a very young age to pray regularly. The second thing she did was to arrange her daughter's marriage. By age two, according to the custom of the time, Elisabeth was betrothed to the eldest son of a local Landgrave – but when his eldest son, Hermann, died, she became betrothed to the second eldest, Ludwig.

Ludwig married Elisabeth in 1221 – he was twenty-one and she was fourteen. Ludwig proposed that they take 'Piety, Chastity, and Justice' as their family motto. They committed themselves as a couple to pray regularly, practice hospitality, and rule justly. In the same year that Ludwig and Elisabeth were married, the Franciscans set up their first base in Germany. And Brother Rodeger, one of the first Germans to become a Franciscan, became Elisabeth's spiritual mentor. He encouraged her to practice the Be-Attitudes.

Elisabeth had brought great wealth and a substantial dowry to her marriage with Ludwig. In the early days she owned so many castles she was called 'Elisabeth of Many Castles'. But as time went by she became increasingly concerned for the poor and began to ride around the countryside to assess the plight of the impoverished among her people. Elisabeth couldn't see the need and not respond to it, so she began distributing alms all over the kingdom. She even gave away the robes of state and the ornaments of office.

Once she started giving, Elisabeth didn't stop at just giving her things. She also looked for ways to give herself. She built a twenty-eight-bed hospital for the poor in Wartburg and visited the patients daily herself. Every day she helped feed nine hundred hungry people. Ludwig and Elisabeth lived such exemplary lives that people started to refer to them as 'St Ludwig' and 'St Elisabeth'.

In 1227 Elisabeth's beloved husband, Ludwig IV, died. The twenty-year-old Elisabeth was inconsolable. 'The world – and all its joys – is now dead to me,' she cried.[34] The next year Elisabeth sent her children to stay with her aunt, formally 'renounced the world', gave away her inheritance, and joined the Franciscans, as the first tertiary (the third order of those that lived under a lay form of the Franciscan Rule) in Hungary. The queen now dedicated herself to the full-time service of beggars. She provided them with clothes, shoes, and agricultural tools. She opened the first orphanage in Eastern Europe for destitute children. And, at the hospice she established in Marburg, she tended to the needs of dying lepers with her own hands – washing the sick and burying the dead. On November 17th, 1231, Elisabeth died. Having received very little support or guidance from her spiritual director, she had become completely worn out by her sacrificial service to the poor. At the tender age of twenty-four, Elisabeth died one of the most influential activists in thirteenth-century Europe.

The political philosopher John Ralston Saul says of Elisabeth,

> She and Francis of Assisi were the most famous
> activists [of their day]. To a great extent they laid
> out the modern democratic model of inclusion –
> an important step towards egalitarianism.
> Elisabeth used her position, as a member of the
> ruling class, to put the ideas into action.

Because of her commitment to the Be-Attitudes, Saul
continues,

> like many others, Elisabeth created a hospice. But
> unlike others, she went beyond pity and charity.
> She washed the sick and buried the dead. It is
> hard to imagine now the public impact of a royal
> figure washing the bodies of the homeless dead.
> Imagine the [president, prime minister] not
> visiting or holding hands with street people, but
> [actually] washing their bodies for burial.

Elisabeth, Saul says, 'took the elements of personal
responsibility, set out tantalisingly in the New Testament,
and imagined a social model which would change our
societies'.[35]

• • •

Vladimir Ilyich Lenin, the (in)famous twentieth-century
revolutionary, reflected on his own life in the light of the
life of his twelfth-century 'comrade', and wrote at the end
of his life: 'I have deluded myself. Without doubt, it was
necessary to free the oppressed masses. However, our
methods resulted in other oppressions and gruesome

massacres. You know I am deathly ill; I feel lost in an ocean of blood formed by countless victims. This was necessary to save our Russia, but it is too late to turn back. We would need ten Francis of Assisi.'[36]

I think Lenin was right on three counts: First, the oppressed need to be liberated. Second, a violent struggle only serves to provoke further violence. Third, the way forward is best represented by brother Francis - and sister Clare. The past cannot be altered. But the future can be. And to change the future - 'without provoking further oppression' - we need to develop movements that will meet the challenge of the coming 'New Dark Age' as faithfully as Francis and Clare did in their day. I believe that, in order for such movements to be faithful, we will need to flesh out the same compassionate spirit embodied in the Be-Attitudes that Francis and Clare did.

Deliver Us From Evil

The final phrase in the prayer Jesus taught his disciples is not an upbeat paean of praise crying aloud - 'for yours is the kingdom, the power, and the glory'. These words, in fact, are not in the original text at all. The final phrase is actually a humble, downbeat petition for help - 'lead us not into temptation, but deliver us from evil'. Edmund Burke is thought to have once said, 'All that is necessary for the triumph of evil, is for good men [and women] to do nothing.' And that is precisely the temptation we all face - the temptation to do nothing, to withdraw, to take it easy, to turn on the television, to make cynical comments about the state of the world and do nothing. Jesus knew from hard personal experience how easy it would be to succumb to the temptation to give up doing good and to decide to go along with evil just to get along. Jesus' challenge is this: 'not to be overcome with evil but to overcome evil with good' (Rom. 12:21) – 'on earth as it is in heaven' (Matt. 6:10).

There are four perspectives that explain the relationship between 'heaven' and 'earth' and explore the possibility of doing God's will 'on earth as it is in heaven'.

The first perspective is the 'traditional perspective'.[37] This perspective sees reality in terms of two parallel dimensions – a 'heavenly' one and an 'earthly' one – which intersect and interact and simultaneously reflect and reinforce the actions of one in the other. From this traditional perspective the 'New Dark Age' could be seen, as it is by Frank Peretti in his best-selling contemporary novels *This Present Darkness* and *Piercing the Darkness*, as 'earthly skirmishes' in a 'heavenly war' between 'God and the Devil'.[38] Certainly people like Martin Luther and John Calvin saw their battles precisely in these terms. Martin Luther said that 'we are all subject to the Devil'.[39] And John Calvin said that the task of every saint is to engage in 'unceasing struggle against the Devil'.[40]

The second perspective is the 'spiritualistic perspective'.[41] Those looking from this perspective see reality in terms of two parallel dimensions – a 'heavenly' one that is manifest in the soul and an 'earthly' one that is manifest in the body. From this point of view the heavenly dimension is 'real' and 'right' while the earthly dimension is either 'unreal' and/or 'wrong'. Baba Ram Dass, in his cult classic *Be Here Now*, sees the 'New Dark Age' from a spiritualistic perspective as nothing but a 'bad dream' from which we will eventually awake to the realization that 'pleasure and pain, loss and gain, fame and shame, are all the same – they're just happening'.[42] Certainly people like the Gnostic Monoimus and Meister Eckhart saw matters precisely in these terms. They believed that 'enlightenment' would dispel the 'ignorance' that produces a 'nightmarish existence' and 'experiences of terror'.[43]

The third perspective, the 'materialistic perspective', is the exact opposite of the spiritualistic perspective.[44] Like the spiritualistic perspective, the materialistic perspective also sees reality in terms of two parallel dimensions – an 'earthly' one that is manifest in the body and a 'heavenly' one that is manifest in the soul. But in this case the earthly dimension is 'real' and 'right', while the heavenly dimension is either 'unreal' and/or 'wrong'. Sigmund Freud, for example, sees the 'New Dark Age' from a materialistic perspective in his famous text *The Future of Illusion* as nothing but 'fulfilments of the oldest, strongest and most urgent wishes of mankind'.[45] Certainly people like Karl Marx and Friedrich Engels saw issues precisely in these terms. They said that the so-called 'religious' character of much of the violence in the world was 'simply a sacred cloak to hide desires that are very secular'.[46]

The fourth perspective is the 'integral perspective'.[47] This perspective sees reality in terms of two coterminous aspects of the universe – an 'outer' or 'earthly' one and an 'inner' or 'heavenly' one – so that every event has both an outer, visible, material aspect as well as an inner, invisible, spiritual aspect. From the integral perspective, the 'New Dark Age' could be seen, as it is by Morton Kelsey in his beautiful book *The Other Side of Silence*, as destructive material expressions of demonic spiritual realities 'that are actually parts of a single realm, [though] at present, they may appear to separate'.[48] Certainly people like Walter Wink and Charles Elliott see the current events precisely in these terms. Walter Wink says that 'institutions have an actual spiritual ethos and we neglect this aspect of institutional life to our peril'.[49] Charles Elliott contends that 'we have to return to the basic position that demonic powers control structures', religious and secular alike, 'and it is those powers that have to be confronted if the structures are to be set free' from their destructive proclivities.[50]

There is probably some truth in all of these views. If the traditional view is true, we need to recognize that there is more going in the world on than meets the eye. If the spiritualistic perspective is true, we need to seek spiritual enlightenment. If the materialistic perspective is true, we need to critique illusion in the name of the spiritual enlightenment that we seek. But if the integral perspective is true, the only way we can guarantee that God's will is 'done on earth as it in heaven' is to exorcise our demonic propensities, embrace our divinely-given potential, and seek to do God's will 'on earth as it in heaven' in the 'power of the Spirit' just like Jesus did.

A Strong but Gentle Power

Jesus said that without the power of the Spirit we should not even try to work for change, lest we end up destroying the world that we are trying to create (Luke 24:49). However, with the Spirit's strong but gentle power, Jesus said, nothing on earth can stop us from embodying the kingdom of heaven on earth – not lack of funds, not lack of numbers – nothing (Matt. 17:20). When Jesus sent his disciples out into the world to incarnate the kingdom of heaven on earth he imparted to them what he called 'the power of the Spirit' (John 20:21–22). This Spirit was 'not a spirit of timidity, but of power, characterized by discipline of self, and compassion for others' (2 Tim. 1:7). So as they opened themselves to this Spirit they received the strong but gentle power to control themselves and to love others as they loved themselves.

Now most people who have been involved in trying to bring about change in the world would find it easy to accept Jesus' idea – that power was the most important single issue in the process. But many would find it more difficult to accept the kind of power – the power of the Spirit – that Jesus advocated. This is not merely because of the spiritual language Christ used to describe the power he advocated, but also because of the substantial difference between the dominant notion of power, to which many of us subscribe, and the alternative notion of power which he advocated.

There are two ways of understanding power. Traditionally we have defined power as the ability to control other people. This dominant notion of power emphasizes the possibility of bringing about change through coercion – by trying to make others change according to our agendas. While this traditional notion entails taking control of our lives by taking control of others, Jesus advocated a radical alternative – taking control of our lives not by taking control of others but by taking control of ourselves. This alternative emphasizes bringing change by conversion. Rather than trying to make others change we try to change ourselves, individually and collectively, in the light of a glorious agenda for justice. This approach breaks the control that others have over us and liberates us from our desire to control others.

The dominant notion of power is popular because it often brings quick, dramatic results. But it is also characterized by short-term gains for some and long-term losses for everyone else. Every violent revolution has always, sooner or later, betrayed the people in whose name the bloody war of liberation was fought. Jesus' alternative notion of power is generally unpopular because it is usually a slow, unspectacular process – but it is also the only way for groups to transcend their selfishness, resolve their conflicts, and manage their affairs in a way that does justice to everyone.

The essential problem in any situation of injustice is this: one human being is exercising control over another and exploiting the relationship of dominance. The solution to the problem is not simply to reverse roles in the hope that once the roles have been reversed the manipulation will discontinue. The solution is for people to stop trying to control each other. All of us, to one degree or another, exploit the opportunity if we have control over another person's life. Common sense therefore dictates that the solution to the problem of exploitation cannot come through controlling others.

The solution, rather, is in the alternative – the strong but gentle approach with attitudes like the Be-Attitudes which emphasize controlling ourselves, individually and collectively, through self-managed processes and structures.

Some of us sincerely believe that if we are to help people, particularly the oppressed, we need to manage their affairs for them. But it doesn't matter how we try to rationalize it – controlling others always empowers us and disempowers those we seek to help.

The only way people, particularly the oppressed, can be helped, is when they are empowered to take control over their own lives. This is why Christ explicitly forbade his followers from taking control over others, no matter how dire the circumstances. Their job was not to seek control over others, but to enable others to take control over their own lives (Matt. 20:25-28).

It is a great irony that the greatest modern example of someone who did act on Christ's advice, and who practiced the Be-Attitudes like few Christians have ever done, did not claim to be a Christian. We need a lot more people who will experiment with the non-violent revolution of '*swaraj*' like Gandhi.

It is a pity that many of us who claim to follow Christ have not followed his advice. We could have been saved the crusades, the inquisitions, and colonial religion.

It's interesting to note that Christ and his disciples used organic images to describe how the power of the Spirit actually produces '*swaraj*', or self-control. The Bible describes self-management as 'the fruit of the Spirit' (Gal. 5:22). The capacity to manage ourselves develops quite unobtrusively – indeed, as quietly as fruit growing on a tree. Like a tiny seed we can scarcely see, the power of the Spirit seems embarrassingly insignificant at first. Yet it grows to have tremendous significance in the end (Matt. 13:31–32). We do not develop the capacity to control our own lives without opposition, but, like a plant growing in the midst of weeds, the power of the Spirit grows strong in an environment that could easily destroy it (Matt. 13:24–30).

How the seeds of transformation that bear the fruit of the Spirit grow always was, and always will be, a mystery (Mark 4:26–29). However, it is no secret that these seeds of transformation will not grow in our community if those of us whose lives constitute the seeds do not bury ourselves in the life of our community. 'Unless a seed falls into the ground and dies it produces nothing, but if it dies it will produce much fruit, that brings much life to others' (John 12:24).

The Be-Attitude Revolution

If we are going to embody the kingdom of heaven on earth there are a few steps that, sooner or later, we all need to take. The first step we all need to take is a step of *integrity*. This is a personal step that we take when we decide that we can live 'divided no more' but want to live by what we believe and practice the Be-Attitudes.[51] The second step we all need to take is a step of *unity*. This is a relational step that we take when we decide that we need to unite with others and work out a way forward to practice the Be-Attitudes together.[52] The third step we all need to take is a step of *solidarity*. This is a political step that we take when we decide that we need to make our private allegiances and private alliances public in order to practice the Be-Attitudes.[53] The fourth step we all need to take is a step of *policy*. This is a structural step that we take when we decide that we need to develop alternative groups and organizations in our communities based on the Be-Attitudes.[54]

However, although these steps seem fairly straightforward and the power of the Spirit is clear, nearly every time I talk with people about developing alternative groups and organizations, the conversation quickly turns from a focus on internal sources we can access through the Spirit to external sources like 'funds' and 'numbers'. If people want to organize a welfare programme, they want to talk about funds. 'Where can we get the funds we need to run the programme?' they inquire. If people want to organize a protest movement, they want to talk numbers. 'How can we get the numbers we need to get a major social movement on a roll?' they ask. These reactions reveal that people on both the right and left of the political spectrum believe that external resources matter more than internal sources of power. They believe that we can only do significant work in our communities if we have access to either lots of cash or large crowds – or both. It's all about fundraising and number crunching.

Because so many people frame their problems, and the solutions to their problems, in terms of access to resources (which, by definition, are beyond their control), they disempower themselves. If they can't get access to the resources they require in order to act, they simply do not act. If they do get the resources they require they may act – but only according to the terms and conditions that have been set for the support they receive. Either way, they abrogate their power to solve their own problems; they project the power to solve their problems onto others; and, in so doing, they render themselves powerless.

Jesus challenged people's dependence on external resources. On two occasions he sent his disciples out into various villages to do some work for his Be-Attitude Revolution. The first time Jesus sent his disciples out into the world he forbade them to take any money at all. According to Jesus, money was not essential. Money was merely a note promising to share a certain amount of commodities or services. What mattered to Jesus was not that his disciples carried a note that held the promise of help, but that they actually practised the Be-Attitudes and helped the people they met out of their own internal resources. The second time Jesus sent his disciples out he allowed them to take a little money – but not much. According to Jesus money was never a primary source, only a secondary one. External resources like money could be helpful as a secondary resource for community work. But when people try to substitute external resources for internal ones, and money becomes a primary, rather than a secondary, consideration – then, Jesus warned us, money will destroy his Be-Attitude Revolution. After all, Paul said, 'the love of money is the source of evil' (1 Tim. 6:10).

On both occasions when Jesus sent his disciples out to do work for his Be-Attitude Revolution he didn't send them out in big numbers. Neither did he expect them to get big numbers involved. It was less a mass movement and more a micro movement. He didn't send his disciples out in their hundreds or thousands but in twos. And he didn't expect them to get hundreds or thousands involved but one here, and one there. As far as Jesus was concerned, two meeting one and forming a group of three was a big enough crowd to begin the Be-Attitude Revolution. For Jesus, a 'trinity' was not so much a theological abstraction as it was a theological strategy for incarnating the kingdom of heaven on earth. A group of three could create within themselves the stability and security necessary for incarnating a kingdom ('A cord of three strands is not easily broken' [Eccl. 4:12]). A group of three could create within themselves both the subjectivity and the objectivity necessary for incarnating a kingdom on earth ('Let every matter be decided on the basis of two or three witnesses'

[Matt. 18:16]). And a group of three could create within themselves the space necessary for incarnating Christ's kingdom of heaven on earth here and now ('Wherever two or three of you gather in my name', Jesus said, 'there am I in the midst of you' [Matt. 18:20*]).

Who are the groups who can incarnate the kingdom of heaven on earth?

- The poor - or poor in spirit - who identify with the poor in spirit

- Those who mourn - who grieve over the injustice in the world

- The meek - who get angry, but who never get aggressive

- Those who hunger and thirst for righteousness - who seek justice

- The merciful - who are compassionate to everyone in need

- The pure in heart - who are wholehearted in their desire to do right

- The peacemakers - who work for peace in a world at war

- Those persecuted for righteousness - who suffer for just causes.

---

* For an in-depth explanation of the 'trinity' as a model for incarnating the Kingdom of Heaven on Earth read the author's latest book *A Divine Society* www.daveandrews.com.au

What are the virtues that these groups need to incarnate in their lives?

- Humility: Focusing on the poor (not status or riches)

- Empathy: Grieving over the injustice in the world

- Self-restraint: Getting angry but not aggressive

- Righteousness: Seeking for justice (not vengeance)

- Mercy: Extending compassion to all in need

- Integrity: Being wholehearted in a desire to do right

- Non-violence: Working for peace in a world at war

- Perseverance: Suffering (patiently) for just causes

If we were to use these virtues, blessed in the Be-Attitudes, as the guidelines for our personal-political lives, just imagine how we could embody the Be-Attitudes.

Stories of Light in Darkness

For the last five years I have been an advisor for Servants to Asia's Urban Poor. Servants is a network of spiritual communities committed to living and working holistically with the poor in Asia's urban slums. Servants has been going for twenty years, and they have developed communities in India, Thailand, Cambodia, and the Philippines. They seek to do whatever they can to be the change they want to see in the world by helping the poorest of the poor. They do everything from developing informal associations of supportive relationships through to developing formal organizations delivering professional community services.

Servants is a modest but important model of a movement that seeks to incarnate the Be-Attitudes in our brutal world through the power of the Spirit.

Let me tell you a couple of stories that show us how to shine a little light in our dark times.

The first story is about Mike and Karen and the Kahawaha Slum.[55] Several years ago Mike and Karen, an Aussie couple, decided it was time for them to take the Be-Attitudes more seriously and respond to the needs of the world's poor more personally and practically. So they decided to go with Servants to India. Upon their arrival in New Delhi in 1999 they began to look around town for a slum in which to live. They found a little hut in the Kahawaha slum, which had been built on government land along the bank of a drainage canal. Together with their young son, they settled in alongside nine hundred other families. Over the next couple of years Mike and Karen immersed themselves in the life of the slum – living alongside the slum-dwellers, learning their language and culture, and developing heaps of reciprocal relationships with their neighbours.

During this time they got to know Amir and Shruti. Amir was born and raised as a Muslim in Kolkata. He became a follower of Jesus as a result of reading Christian literature he confiscated at a checkpoint when the Operation Mobilisation driver refused to pay a bribe. Amir's wife, Shruti, was born and raised as a Hindu. After becoming a follower of Jesus, she met and married Amir and they went together to study at the Bible college. When Amir and

Shruti returned home they met with angry reactions – particularly from the local Muslim community of which Amir had once been a part. A *fatwah*, or order to kill, was issued against Amir as an infidel. Amir and Shruti had to flee, so they made their way to New Delhi. They arrived with nothing and spent the first month living on the platform of the New Delhi railway station. After that Amir and Shruti moved into a *basti* in a nearby slum, where they found many other Urdu-speaking migrants and refugees. They felt a call to work in slums where there were significant numbers of 'their people', so Amir and Shruti began working in one of the largest slum colonies in Delhi. Mike and Karen offered to help Amir and Shruti develop their work and were given the task of documenting the basic needs of the people in the slum.

In the slum there was a total population of 135,000 destitute people in 13,200 *basti* shacks. There was no government water supply to the area, so all the water for the slum came from hand pumps. Diarrhoea and dysentery were common. Residents also regularly suffered from malaria because they lived so close to the river. A government survey in 1997 suggested that the male literacy rate in the area was five per cent and the female literacy rate was two per cent.

Amir and Shruti asked Mike and Karen to help them develop a project proposal that Himmat – their emerging local community organization – could submit for funding. The proposal was approved, and the project began. Over time Himmat has helped people in the colony rebuild their houses after fires, then floods, then fires again swept through the slums. They have trained twelve community health workers; started sixteen classes for children and thirty-two for adults; organized eighty micro-finance co-ops; and begun sixteen house churches.

On October 19th, 2001, someone pointed a notice out to Mike that had been pasted onto the communal toilet block. It said that the council was going to clear the slum in six days and relocate the people twenty-five kilometres away. Understandably, the people were distraught. Mike called several community meetings to discuss the eviction. After hearing all who wanted to contribute, the people decided they needed to get: 1) a stay order until winter was over, which would give them time to raise the deposit to buy new land in the relocation area; 2) legal title to the new land before the relocation took place; and 3) legal entitlement to new land for all of the people in the slum who owned huts.

Mike, who is a lawyer by training, had identified a group of local lawyers who could take the case to the Delhi High Court. He liaised between the representatives of the slum and the lawyers and, eventually, they got the backing of the court for the slum-dwellers' basic demands. During the hearings, a judge asked for a list of the families in the slum but the council refused to make their list available. So Mike and his friends in the slum had to embark on the huge logistical task of making another list of all the families in the slum.

Chotu was one of Mike's friends in the slum who'd offered to help. The two of them, with the help of some other friends, set about the task of collecting all the information.

Chotu's hut became the centre of operations where they documented everyone's name, ration card, hut number, and entitlement. After weeks of hard work, Chotu and Mike had an up-to-date list that helped ensure the entitlement of a dozen or more families who were eligible but would have otherwise missed out in the allotment.

Mike was dropping his son off at school one day when he saw literally hundreds of armed police in riot gear getting ready to forcefully clear the slum. Mike borrowed a friend's mobile phone and contacted everyone he knew in order to stop the provocation and the inevitable violence that would result from the fighting that would follow the police action. Fortunately, the police force was recalled to the barracks at the last minute and the relocation was deferred. Subsequently Mike and his friends were able to negotiate the peaceful relocation of the people. In the end they got land entitlements for more than eighty per cent of the slum-dwellers – some seven hundred and fifty families.

In the new location the people soon discovered, however, that there was no water, no electricity, next to no transport, and their new land was three to five feet lower than the road so, when it rained, it flooded and became a dirty great big swamp. Mike and his friends had to go back to court with the lawyers again and again to negotiate building up the level of the land and the provision of drinking water and electricity. There are still not enough buses. The struggle of the Be-Attitudes goes on.

In the meantime, Mike, Karen, and Chotu are working together with Amir and Shruti and Himmat and a range of other local agencies to provide small loans to help the people start some small businesses. Mike is also writing a pamphlet in Urdu on a protocol for relocating slum-dwellers, in the hope that it will be used to inform people of their rights in future forced relocations in the city.

· · ·

Mike, Karen, Chotu, and their friends Amir and Shruti in Himmat, are shining examples of the light of God's love in the midst of our current darkness. But not all of us will be able to pack up our bags and join a team in New Delhi, Kolkata, Bangkok, Manila, or Phnom Penh. If this is the case in your life my next story - about Peter and Adrienne and the Cabramatta Gardens - is just for you.

Peter and his wife Adrienne wanted to go to work in Vietnam. But, as often happens, things didn't work out the way they had hoped they would. So instead of moving to Hanoi this Kiwi couple decided that they would move to Sydney and work with the Vietnamese community in Cabramatta.

When they arrived in Cabramatta, Peter and Adrienne joined Urban Concern, a faith community that was supportive of Servants work - not just overseas, but back home as well, encouraging people to practice the Be-Attitudes in our own backyards. Through Urban Concern Peter and Adrienne were introduced to Cabramatta and soon got to know not only the Vietnamese there but also Cambodians and refugees from former Yugoslavia as well. The whole world was on their doorstep.

In late 1999 Peter and his friends began to discuss the idea of 'doing something together' in the community. By January 2000 this vague notion of 'doing something together' had evolved into the idea of a community garden. By February they had identified the Hughes Street Playground as the preferred site and in April submitted a formal proposal to lease a portion of the site.

Now the Hughes Street Playground was a notorious place. It had been taken over by the 'smack squad' a long time ago. But Peter and his friend Jeremy thought it was the perfect place for local people to begin to take back some of their space and put it to good, sustainable community use. They were not only given permission to use Hughes Street, but they also received a $10,000 grant from the Fairfield City Council to fund the initial set-up of the garden. They worked with a group of local representatives over a twelve-month period on the details of how to proceed with the project.

The group came up the idea of having an 'Open Day' to share the dream of the garden with the community and to invite people of various ethnic backgrounds – especially those people on the 'margins' – to join in and work on the project together. Invitations were given out in seven different languages through community radio and a letter-box drop, and about two hundred people turned up for the Open Day in March 2001. Ninety people filled in forms with their suggestions. In June there was an excursion to other community gardens around town. In August there was a training day on 'organic gardening'. And October saw the first on-site workday. So by December 2001 the first eight plots were planted – and by January 2002 the first crops were harvested. By July 2002, all twenty-three plots had been completed and allocated. The construction of the garden has been dependent on the people in the project who are prepared to work for the benefit of the whole garden – not just their own patch. A committee of three people has been elected, from each of the three language groups represented, to manage the project.

The garden has been a great success on a number of significant levels. It has restored the park. The play area that had fallen into disuse is now being used again by families. The plots are fully subscribed and well maintained and people can gather fresh herbs and vegetables on a daily basis. Moreover, the garden provides a productive, therapeutic occupation for a group of retired, unemployed, or underemployed Cabramatta migrants and refugees. It also provides a safe place for people to forge reciprocal relationships of acceptance and respect across the cross-cultural divide – a symbol of what many of us believe is the 'community of heaven on earth'.

Peter and Adrienne show us that we don't need to be stars in order to be light – all we need to do is to reflect the light of God's love in our lives. We need to simply think of the 'good things' we can do that can bring some light into the darkness – and we need to keep on doing them come what may. It doesn't matter whether these 'good things' we do are big or small. What matters is that we embody the Be-Attitudes.

Lighting a candle is better than cursing the dark.

• • •

Jacques Ellul, the great twentieth-century French sociologist and prophetic voice, once said: 'At the present moment, we are confronted with a choice – the "Brave New World" of Huxley – or a different civilization, which we cannot yet describe because we do not know what it will be; it is still to be created.'[56]

It's our choice. What kind of world do we want to be created in us and through us? The 'Brave New World' or something like 'the Kingdom of Heaven on Earth'? Mike and Karen and Peter and Adrienne show us ways we can humbly seek to embody the Be-Attitudes in our ordinary everyday lives and, in so doing, how we can flesh out the 'the Kingdom of Heaven on Earth' in our world.

Conclusion

Resources
for Your Own
Do-It-Yourself
Be-Attitude
Revolution

To Be or Not to Be: The Challenge

In an article called 'Cold Turkey', the famous satirical American author Kurt Vonnegut wrote: 'For some reason, the most vocal Christians among us never mention the Beatitudes. But – often with tears in their eyes – they demand that the Ten Commandments be posted in public buildings. And of course that's Moses, not Jesus. I haven't heard one of them demand that the Sermon on the Mount, the Beatitudes, be posted anywhere.' Well, I think it's time we took up his challenge and posted the Be-Attitudes everywhere we can.

I'm mindful of how Luther's act of nailing his Ninety-Five Theses for reform to the door of his church led to the reformation of his times. And I believe that posting copies of the Be-Attitudes – not only in private spaces, like on the backs of our bedroom doors, but also in public spaces, like on the front doors of our churches – might lead to a new, and more radical, reformation. This reformation would not only preach grace as a precept but also practice it as a process.

Imagine what could happen if, instead of merely reciting our creeds, which (by and large) have little ethical content, we began every week by reciting and reflecting on the Be-Attitudes, with a focus on Christlike ethical responses?

Imagine what could happen if our churches, temples, synagogues, and mosques were transformed into spirited support groups that were committed to helping people live out the Be-Attitudes as an integrated step program? What AA groups have done for our addiction to alcohol, Be-

Attitude groups could do for our addiction to status and violence. They could set us free to be fully human, fully alive, and fully active in loving our neighbours as ourselves!

To Be or Not to Be: The Call

We are inviting you to help us help one another to be the people we can be by:

- Discovering and/or creating as many different beautiful versions of the Be-Attitudes as we can

- Posting your favourite version of the Be-Attitudes in a private space where you can see it – like on the back of your bedroom door

- Posting your favourite version of the Be-Attitudes in a public space where others can see it – like on the front door of your church

- Posting your favourite version of the Be-Attitudes on the wecan.be website

- Signing the pledge on the website to practice the Be-Attitudes

- Meditating, acting, reflecting on the Be-Attitudes yourself

- Sharing your own experiences through the wecan.be website

- Sending in quotes, songs, and images that inspired you to the wecan.be website so that others can 'be inspired'

- Sending in stories, including your own, so others can 'be encouraged'

- Sending in news, views, articles, and editorials so others can 'be informed'

- Sending in the names of groups of potential partners to 'be connected'

- Sending in the details of campaigns for peace and justice to 'be active'

- Sending in meditations to help us 'be reflective'

- Using the wecan.be buttons, postcards, and T-shirts to engage others.

Remember: we cannot change others. We can only change ourselves. Let's commit ourselves to embodying the Be-Attitudes as best we can in our ordinary everyday lives and 'be the change we want to see in the world'.

Credo's Be-Attitudes

Blessed are the battlers who, through their struggle,
are open about who they really are
and see the deception of wealth.
They will understand that, in God's way,
there is enough for all.
Those who are grieved by the way of the world,
who see that things aren't right, will be blessed.
Although they will be told to 'get over it'
they will find hope together.
Those who are compassionate and humble,
putting others before themselves, will be blessed.
They will understand their place in creation.
'Ya chasin'?'
The only real hit is to sort things out
with the world around you and God who created you.

A user got ripped off in a deal.
Soon after he found the dealer overdosed
in the Baptist Place laneway by himself.
Although the user wanted revenge in 'street justice',
he called the ambos and got help from Credo
to keep him alive
not even checking his pockets to steal his gear or cash.
This is mercy. Be like this and you will be shown mercy.
People who are honest and open like children
are blessed.
They will see God.

A drunk man in Credo was abusing people
serving the meal
when a young streety came up to him and said:
'Hey man, this is a good place, it's a church, it's not evil.'
When the drunk man heard this he gave the streety
a hug and settled down.
Those who make peace are children of God.

When you try to do things right,
some people around you will think that you're weird
and give you a hard time . . .
Like Uncle Vincent Lingari
who stood up for the rights and land of his people
but was laughed at and told that it would never happen.
He had to camp out
and wait for seven years
before he and his people were listened to.

Like someone who has given up heroin
and still gets called a junkie
and is hassled by the jacks when he comes to town.

Like Jesus who simply loved people
and tried to teach them how to live
and was beaten and killed for it.

If you persevere, God will reward you
with all that is right.[57]

The Be-Attitudes: A Creed

We believe in God . . .
who cherishes the poor
and offers them the riches
of the Commonwealth of God
who hears the sobbing of the sorrowful
and provides them with undying comfort
who sees those who tread softly and humbly
and gives them the earth to look after
who satisfies the hungry and thirsty
with the hospitality of the choicest Table
who honours the merciful
and shows them the fullness of the mercy of God
who recognises pure hearts
and invites them to look upon the glory of God
who strengthens the peacemakers
and names them the free children of God
who suffers with the persecuted
and promises them the freedom of the City of God.
Praise God.[58]

The Be-Attitudes: A Statement of Beliefs

We believe it is a blessing
to be counted amongst the poor
for to such belong the kingdom of God.

It is a blessing to go hungry now
for then we will know satisfaction.

It is a blessing to weep now
for then we will learn how to laugh.

It is a blessing to be hated by people,
insulted by them because of the Son of Man,
for that is how they treated the prophets.

We believe it is not a blessing to be rich
for this is all the comfort we receive.

It is not a blessing to be well fed now
for we will soon hunger.

It is not a blessing to laugh now
for we will mourn and weep later.

It is not a blessing to have all people speak well of us
for that is how they treated the false prophets.

We believe in loving our enemies and
doing good to those who persecute us,
blessing those who curse us and
praying for those who mistreat us.

We believe in turning the other cheek,
giving away that which others would take from us,
doing to others as we would have them do to us,
lending to 'sinners' without expecting anything back.

We believe in being merciful,
being kind to those who are ungrateful and wicked,
for our reward in heaven is enormous.

We believe in refusing to judge,
lest we in turn be judged,
refusing to condemn, so we will not be condemned,
forgiving as we have been forgiven,
giving as we have received.

We believe in attending to our own blindness
before addressing the short-sightedness in others,
bearing good fruit
and putting the words of Jesus into practice.[59]

The Be-Attitudes: A Benediction

Blessed are the poor . . .
not the penniless, but those free from love of money.

Blessed are those who mourn . . .
not those who whimper, but those who raise their
voices.

Blessed are the meek . . .
not those who are wimpy, but those who are patient
and tolerant

Blessed are those who hunger and thirst for justice . . .
not those who whine, but those who struggle for
change.

Blessed are the merciful . . .
not those who forget, but those who still forgive.

Blessed are the pure in heart . . .
not those who act like angels, but those who are
transparent.

Blessed are the peacemakers . . .
not those who shun conflict, but those who face it
creatively.

Blessed are those who are persecuted for justice . . .
not because they suffer, but because they love
courageously.[60]

The Be-Attitudes: A Prayer

Lord, grant me
the serenity
To accept the people I cannot change,
The courage to change the one I can,
And the wisdom to know it is me!

The Be-Attitudes: A Pledge

I Want to Be the Change I Want to See . . .

I will identify with the poor 'in spirit'.

I will grieve over injustice in the world.

I will get angry, but never get aggressive.

I will seek to do justice, even to my enemies.

I will extend compassion to all those in need.

I will act with integrity, not for the publicity.

I will work for peace in the midst of violence.

I will suffer myself, rather than inflict suffering.

Signed...................................... Date.............

Warning:
We need to take the Be-Attitudes seriously,
but we shouldn't take ourselves too seriously.

The Be-Attitudes: A Songbook

1. Jesus' Song (The Be-Attitudes)[61]

The sun rose early; climbed into the sky;
Took away the cold night air;
brought the warm dawn light.

And Jesus sat upon a rock,
Looking round at the gathering throng
Who came to the mount to hear him speak –
to hear him sing his song.

Many were sick; many there were sore;
Many of them were desperate; many of them were poor.

Tho' you feel lost – God's always gonna be with you,
Tho' you feel sad – his grace is gonna see you through.
Don't lose your temper –
'cause in the end you're gonna win this fight.
Always strive for justice – everything's gonna be alright.

When you show mercy – then mercy will be shown to you.
Act with integrity – and you'll see your vision come true.
Where you solve conflict –
they'll call you the 'children of God'.
Some people may hate you – but the love of God is yours.

2. Love Reigns (Micah 6:8; 1 John 3:17–18)[62]

He has showed you all – what is good.
And what does the Lord require of you?
To justly act, with mercy to love
To humbly walk with your God

So let us love! Let us love!
Not in words or speech, but in truth and in deed
When a brother or sister is in need . . .

In the Kingdom of Friends.
In the Kingdom of Friends.

So give of your heart. Give of Your mind.
Give of your soul. Give what you find.
Give of your time. Give of your wealth
Give as if Jesus was giving himself.

In the Kingdom of Friends – Love reigns!
In the Kingdom of Friends – Love reigns!

3. Christ that Bleeds: The Crux – Part One[63]

Standing here at the foot of the cross. I see life as it is . . .
The flesh flayed raw. The crowd cry more.
The wounds that weep.

Some of us would kill for hire; some of us kill for desire;
Some of us would kill for fear; some of us kill for power.

We crucify with sophistry. We crucify with style.
We crucify with bigotry. We crucify with bias.
We crucify with pleasantries. We crucify with smiles.
We crucify with treacheries. We crucify with lies.

At the crux of this tragedy, it's painfully clear to see . . .
If we crucify even the least – it's Christ that bleeds.

4. What Love Is This? The Crux – Part Two[64]

Strung out - naked - on the cross
- assaulted by our age.
We see the cuts. We hear the cries.
You suffer our disgrace.

Around your brows form lines of kindness.
In your eyes there's care.
Down your cheeks flow tears of sadness.
On your lips - a prayer.

What love is this - as strong as death -
that lives life as it should?
What love is this - with its last breath -
sets bad aside for good?

Love never looked so sorrowful.
Love never looked so sore.
Love never looked so beautiful.
Love never looked so pure.
Love never looked so remarkable.
Love never looked so great.
Love never looked so lovable.
As it looks - upon your face.

5. The Way of Christ: The Crux – Part Three[65]

'This is my body broken for you.
This is my blood that I shed.
Do it to . . . the least of these . . .
In memory of me.'

There's no faith where there is no grace.
No grace where no sacrifice.
No way – but the way of Christ –
A love that lays down its life. *(x2)*

No other way but redemption.
No other way but prayer.
No other way but compassion.
No other way but care.
No other way but devotion.
No other way but love.
No other way but dedication.
No other way but the cross.

There's no faith where there is no grace.
No grace where no sacrifice.
No way – but the way of Christ –
A love that lays down its life. *(x2)*

6. Sorry[66]

I was told that we were the good guys – a long time ago.
I was told that we fought the good fight – from go to woe.
I was told that we wrote the guidelines – to give a fair go.
I was told that we'd always do right – by friend and foe

Sorry, Aussies, I don't think that no more!
Sorry, Aussies, I think we're against what we say we're for!

I was told we'd sort out inequity – not let it go.
I was told we'd strive for equality – for young and old.

Sorry, Murries,* I don't think that no more!
Sorry, Murries, I think we're against what we say we're for!

I was told we'd vote for a demagogue – to hit the road.
I was told we'd welcome the underdog – bring 'em home.

Sorry, Refugees, I don't think that no more!
Sorry, Refugees, I think we're against what we say we're for!

I was told we'd protect the innocent – from brutal terror.
I was told we'd care for civilians – in event of war.

Sorry, Iraqis, I don't think that no more!
Sorry, Iraqis, I think we're against what we say we're for!

Sorry. So sorry.

* An indigenous word for Aborigines in South East
 Queensland where I live.

7. Hey-Hey You Say: The Lord's Prayer[67]

Hey-hey we say, that 'You are my God!'
Hey-hey we say, 'My God, you're good!'
Hey-hey we say, 'I'm prayin' for the day –
that I can live life like I should.'

Hey-hey you say, 'Let's end the war!'
Hey-hey you say, 'Let's feed the poor!'
Hey-hey you say, 'Let's make a start today –
to live a life worth living for.'

'May your kingdom come –
with love for everyone –
on earth, as it is in heaven!'

Hey-hey you say, 'Let's end the war!'
Hey-hey you say, 'Let's feed the poor!'

8. Don't Be Afraid[68]

Fearful - we're fearful of others.
Fearful of contact with people -
unless they're just like us.
Fearful - we're fearful of difference.
Fearful of conflict with strangers -
who ain't the same as us.

(But) God's embrace is great.
His amazing grace never fails to save.
God's love conquers hate
- so don't be afraid. (x2)

Fearful - we're fearful of changes.
Fearful of fighting -
Fearful of winning - fearful of loss.
Fearful - we're fearful of dangers.
Fearful of following a leader -
who died on a cross.

Don't be afraid . . .

9. We Can.Be[69]

I can't be a saviour – rescue culture from captivity.
In my soul I know that it's just not me.
I can't be a hero – change the course of history.
But here and now – I can be the me I'm called to be.

Be the kind of person I would like to be.
Though at times it ain't as easy as it seems.

Be the sign of peace that I would like to see.
Thru' the Spirit, inside of me, who inspires me.

I can be. You can be. We can be the way we'd like to be.
I can be. You can be. We can be the world we'd like to see.

The Be-Attitudes: A Booklist

There are a range of books you could read that will help you 'be the revolution'. Some of the books I have written that you might find helpful include *Plan Be, Hey Be and See, See What I Mean?, People of Compassion, Christi-Anarchy, Not Religion but Love* and *Compassionate Community Work*.

Plan Be

'Plan Be is a simple practical easy-to-use manual for a do-it-yourself global ethical revolution. In eight concise punchy chapters Dave Andrews unpacks the hidden dynamics in the eight Be-Attitudes and shows us how they can help us reshape our personal-political worlds.'
–Eden.co.uk

Hey, Be and See

'Dave writes with a wealth of experience on issues that are dear to my heart.' Dave shows 'how we can live our lives prophetically in the context of our times.'
– Jim Wallis, Editor, Sojourners

See What I Mean?

In these stories a touch of heaven comes to earth! Dave shares with wisdom, humour and disarming frankness. We experience his fear, doubts and struggles. We share in the simple joy of seeing those he meets discover life through Christ. These brilliant life stories inspire us to take the Beatitudes at face value and simply do as Jesus asks. The neighbourly reconciliation work felt like something even I could do!
– Matthew Frost, Chief Executive, Tearfund UK

Christi-Anarchy

'[In] this courageous and provocative study . . . Dave Andrews attacks Christian complacency and calls us back to the non-violent, yet radically subversive, 'Way' of Jesus. . . . [*Christi-Anarchy* is] likely to earn applause from some, brickbats from others, but . . . [it is] certain to challenge, and to stimulate serious reflection.'
–Patricia Harrison, Professor, Tabor College

Not Religion but Love

'There is a genius to this book in the way it has been written. If you are looking for quotes, the powerful punchlines come thick and fast. At the end of each chapter is a section for ideas, meditation, discussion and action, which makes it a great tool for living prophetically as people of hope.'
–John Uren, Dean, Whitley College

Compassionate Community Work

'This is a must-read book for all people who want to see their communities revitalized and shaped by Kingdom values. In the process we will be changed as we authentically relate to people around us. It is doable and Dave shows us how. And this is what mission is all about!'
–Ross Coleman, Director of Hope Street

People of Compassion

This is a collection of 40 stories about ordinary people throughout history who have embodied Christ's extraordinary spirit of compassion. The book is intended as a starting point for group discussion or individual reflection on what it means to follow Christ's commandment to love our neighbour. Each story is short, easy to read, and has a few questions for discussion or reflection at the end.

– Naomi Waldron, Review, Journey Magazine

The Wecan.be Website

To enable us to help one another 'be the revolution', we have set up a website: www.wecan.be (donated by some generous Belgians). The general aim of the website is to encourage one another to be the change we want to see in the world. The specific objective of the website is to encourage each other to adopt 'Plan Be' and practice the 'Be-Attitudes'. The explicit strategy is to use a web-based network to encourage one another to adopt 'Plan Be' and practice the 'Be-Attitudes' and share our experiments in the change 'wecan.be'. We want to take as our texts the Be-Attitudes in Matthew 5:1-12 (and Luke 6:20-26) and as our mantra we take a quote from Mahatma Gandhi: 'We must be the change we want to see in the world.'

Specifically, there are six ways we'd like people to help one another through the website. We want people to:

1. 'Be inspired' - through songs, images, quotes, etc.
2. 'Be encouraged' - through stories from around the world
3. 'Be informed' - through current news and views
4. 'Be connected' - through groups we may accompany or who may accompany us on the journey
5. 'Be active' - through practical campaigns
6. 'Be reflective' - through spirited meditations.

We look forward to receiving quotes, songs, and images to 'be inspired'; stories (including your own) to 'be encouraged'; news, views, articles, and editorials to 'be informed'; names of groups of potential partners to 'be connected'; details of campaigns for peace, love, justice, and sustainability to 'be active'; and lots of meditations to help us to 'be reflective'.

Our prayer is that we can be the 'people-that-be' over against the 'powers-that-be'.

The Plan Be Campaign Materials

The Plan Be Campaign is a campaign to reclaim the Be-Attitudes as a creative framework for engaging a world of poverty and violence.

We believe that if we follow the eightfold path of Jesus, according to the Spirit of Jesus, it can be a simple practical step by step guide to our own personal-political revolution.

And when a significant number of us begin to live the Be-Attitudes, and vote the Be-Attitudes, our politicians will follow the people's lead and enact more policies of peace and justice.

- We want to encourage Churches to read the Be-Attitudes every Sunday.

- We want to encourage all Christians to learn the Be-Attitudes by heart.

- We want to encourage each person to select a Be-Attitude to practice.

- We want to encourage people to get together in 'Be-Attitude' Groups to support one another in 'being the change we want to see in the world.'

The Bible Society where I live has agreed to support the Plan Be Campaign and has produced a great range of excellent materials for the Plan Be Campaign.

These include

The Plan Be DVD   – with a one minute promo on the Be-Attitudes

                                   – and 8 vox pop interviews on the 8 Be-Attitudes

The Good Be Guide   – a guide for Be-Attitude Groups or Be Groups

Daily.Be   – an 8 week action guide for the 8 Be-Attitudes

And beautifully designed Plan Be banners, brochures and booklets etc.

These materials are available from the Qld Bible Society at www.bsqld.org.au and we are hoping that in time other Bible Societies will source them too.

Notes

1 Luke 17:21

2 Quoted by Victor Gollancz in From *Darkness to Light* (Bungay: Richard Clay, 1964), p. 297.

3 Quoted by Emilie Griffin in *Wilderness Time* (San Francisco: Harper, 1997), p. 99.

4 Northrop Frye, ed., *Selected Poetry and Prose of William Blake* (Toronto: Random House, 1953), p. 37.

5 Paul's gospel is also a gospel of 'the kingdom of God'. In Acts (19:8; 28:23; 28:30) we hear Paul preaching 'the kingdom', and in his letters we see Paul writing about 'the kingdom' more than 15 times.

6 Brian McLaren, *Everything Must Change* (Nashville: Thomas Nelson, 2007), p. 177.

7 For a detailed study of these Be-Attitudes, read *Plan Be*.

8 Their names have been changed here to protect their identities.

9 Jürgen Moltmann, *The Church in the Power of the Spirit: A Contribution to Messianic Ecclesiology* (Minneapolis: Augsburg Fortress, 1993), pp. 301, 302.

10 Moltmann, *The Church in the Power*, p. 295.

11 Parker Palmer, *Let Your Life Speak* (San Francisco: Jossey-Bass, 2000), p. 49.

12 Palmer, *Let Your Life Speak*, pp. 32-34.

13 Palmer, *Let Your Life Speak*, p. 16.

14 John MacMurray, *Freedom in the Modern World* (London: Faber & Faber, 1958), pp. 28-29, 55.

15 MacMurray, *Freedom*, pp. 88-90.

16 MacMurray, *Freedom*, pp. 58-59.

17 John V. Taylor, *The Go-Between God* (London: SCM Press, 1972), p. 243.

18 Taylor, *The Go-Between God*, p. 243.

19 Wayne Muller, *Legacy of the Heart: The Spiritual Advantages of a Painful Childhood* (Wichita, KS: Fireside, 1993), p. 27 (Isa. 40:13).

20 David Benner, *Surrender to Love: Discovering the Heart of Christian Spirituality* (Downers Grove: InterVarsity, 2003), pp. 84-5.

21 Muller, *Legacy of the Heart,* p. 27.

22 Benner, *Surrender to Love*, pp. 93-4.

23 Desmond Tutu, 'Desmond Tutu's Recipe for Peace' www.beliefnet.com 2004.

24 Jacques Attali, *Millennium* (New York: Random House, 1991), pp. 74-8.

25 Zbigniew Brzezinski, *The Grand Chessboard* (New York: Basic Books), 1997.

26 Ghassan Hage, *Against Paranoid Nationalism* (Annandale: Pluto Press, 2003), p. 20.

27 Hage, *Against Paranoid Nationalism*, p. 18.

28 Hage, *Against Paranoid Nationalism*, p. 20.

29 Hage, *Against Paranoid Nationalism*, p. 140.

30 Hage, *Against Paranoid Nationalism*, p. 20.

31 Bruce Lincoln, *Holy Terrors* (Chicago: University of Chicago Press, 2002).

32 Greg Austin, Todd Kranock, and Thom Oommen, *God and War* (Bradford: Department of Peace Studies, 2003).

33 J.A. Haught, *Holy Horrors* (Buffalo: Prometheus, 1990), pp. 25-26.

34 'Elisabeth of Many Castles', Christian History Institute www.chi.gospelcom.net.

35 John Ralston Saul, *On Equilibrium* (Camberwell: Penguin, 2001), pp. 136-38.

36 www.franciscanfriarstor.com/stfrancis/
    stf_thomas_of_celano_writes.htm.

37 Saul, *On Equilibrium*, p. 4

38 F. Peretti, *This Present Darkness* (Westchester: Crossways
    Books, 1986), and *Piercing the Darkness* (Westchester:
    Crossways Books, 1988).

39 B.P. Levack, *The Witch-Hunt in Early Modern Europe*
    (London: Longman, 2nd ed., 1995), p. 97.

40 Levack, *The Witch-Hunt*, p. 97.

41 W. Wink, *Engaging the Powers: Discernment and Resistance
    in a World of Domination* (Minneapolis: Augsburg Fortress,
    1992), p. 4.

42 R. Alpert, *Be Here Now* (San Cristobal, NM: Lama
    Foundation, 1971), p. 107.

43 H. Ellerbe, *The Dark Side of Christian History* (San Rafael,
    CA: Morningstar & Lark, 1995), p. 12.

44 Wink, *Engaging the Powers*, p. 5.

45 S. Freud, *The Future of Illusion* (London: Hogarth, 1961), p.
    30.

46 K. Marx, *'Debates on Freedom of the Press' Early Texts*
    (Oxford: Oxford University Press, 1971), p. 35.

47 Wink, *Engaging the Powers*, p. 6.

48 M. Kelsey, The Other Side of Silence (New York: Paulist
    Press, 1976), p. 147.

49 Wink, *Engaging the Powers*, p. 6.

50 C. Elliott, *Comfortable Compassion* (London: Hodder &
    Stoughton, 1987), p. 153.

51 Parker Palmer, *The Courage to Teach: Exploring the Inner
    Landscape of a Teacher's Life* (San Francisco: Jossey-Bass,
    1997), p. 167.

52 Palmer, *The Courage to Teach*, p. 172.

53 Palmer, *The Courage to Teach*, p. 175.

54 Palmer, *The Courage to Teach*, p. 180.

55 All the names in these true stories have been changed to protect people's privacy.

56 Jacques Ellul, *The Presence of the Kingdom* (New York: Seabury, 1967), p. 42.

57 Posted by Marcus Curnow, December 22, 2004 http://www.urbanseed.org/journal/mt/mc/archives/2004/12/credo_beatitude.hml.

58 Bruce Prewer, in *Be Our Freedom, Lord: Responsive Prayers and Readings for Contemporary Worship* (ed. Terry Falla; Adelaide: Open Book, 1994).

59 Reflections based on Luke 6:20–49 by Garry Hills.

60 Adapted from A. Cadwallder, B. Kiley, and P. Lockwood, *Give Me Shelter* (Adelaide: Open Book, 2001).

61 Dave Andrews, *Songs of Grace and Struggle* (Brisbane: Frank Communications, 2007). CDs can be purchased on-line from www.lastfirst.net. Lyrics and chords for all songs are available for free from www.daveandrews.com.au. The music can be downloaded in mp3s for free from www.daveandrews.com.au. Any enquiries about these songs can be directed to dandrews@thehub.com.au.

62 Steve Bevis, *Songs of Grace and Struggle* (Brisbane: Frank Communications, 2007).

63 Dave Andrews, *Songs of Grace and Struggle*.

64 Dave Andrews, *Songs of Grace and Struggle*.

65 Dave Andrews, *Songs of Grace and Struggle*

66 Dave Andrews, *Songs of Love and Justice* (Brisbane: Frank Communications, 2006).

67 Dave Andrews, *Songs of Hope and Protest*.

68 Dave Andrews, *Songs of Grace and Struggle*.

69 Dave Andrews and Peter B., *Songs of Hope and Protest*.